Lift Up Your Hearts

Meditations for Those Who Mourn

Mauryeen O'Brien, O.P.

ACTA
ASSISTING CHRISTIANS TO ACT
PUBLICATIONS

Lift Up Your Hearts
Meditations for Those Who Mourn
by Mauryeen O'Brien, O.P.

Edited by John Van Bemmel
Cover design by Tom A. Wright
Typesetting by Garrison Publications

The poem "Good Morning, God" by Vincent Marquis, Wallingford, Connecticut, is used with permission. All rights reserved.

Material on the "four tasks of mourning" are based on the work of J. William Worden as found in his book *Grief Counseling and Grief Therapy,* (c) 1991, Springer Publishing Company, 536 Broadway, New York, NY 10012. All rights reserved.

Bible quotations from the *New Revised Standard Version,* copyright © 1989 by the Division of Christian Education of the National Council of the Churches of Christ in the USA are used with permission. All rights reserved.

Published by: ACTA Publications
Assisting Christians To Act
4848 N. Clark Street
Chicago, IL 60640-4711
800-397-2282

Library of Congress Catalog Number: 00-106105
ISBN: 0-87946-214-0
Printed in the United States of America
Year: 05 04 03 02 01   Printing: 8 7 6 5 4 3 2

Contents

To the memory of
my sister-in-law, Pat,
and to her husband, Brian
and their family,
who together have struggled
through the journey of grief.

Introduction

What is the role of prayer when we grieve the loss of someone we love? Is prayer an integral part of the mourning process? How are we, the bereaved, to pray when our life has suddenly been torn apart? Is prayer even possible at such a time? Certainly, answers to these questions will differ, depending on the personality, the level of faith, and the circumstances of the individual experiencing the pain of grief.

Yet it has been well established that prayer, no matter what form it takes, can be a most comforting and meaningful part—some would insist a necessary part—of the healing process we know as grieving. Lamenting the loss of a loved one by engaging in spiritual activity may be a process we humans must go through if we are ever to be healed.

We know that saying good-bye to loved ones is an integral part of normal, everyday human existence. They may be going off to work, leaving on a vacation, returning to school. If the good-bye is for an extended or indefinite period, we often wonder if we can endure the separation. In a real sense, we don't; a part of us always goes with the person who leaves. Even though moving far away from us may be beneficial to the one we have known and loved—an opportunity for growth and new challenges—it's difficult, even heartbreaking, to say good-bye. ("Good-bye" comes from the expression "God be with you;" it started as a blessing, or prayer, that God would accompany a person on a journey.)

In the case of death, when our good-bye is painfully final, we are left with the sorrow of separation for the rest of our life. Perhaps that is the challenge in the deeply emotional good-bye we express when someone we love dies. Maybe at such a time what we need to work toward is not just *saying* good-bye but *praying* good-bye—allowing the God who travels with us in life and death to make a difference, not only for the one who has died but also for the one left behind. Through our process of grieving we can permit the natural human pattern of saying good-bye to surface so that new life in some form can be reborn in us, so that the death of our loved one can become an

enriching spiritual experience. Is this possible? Yes! Is it difficult? Yes, very much so!

How is any kind of prayer possible at such a time? How do
we pray when we are anesthetized with grief, absorbed in our
emptiness? Perhaps if we allow ourselves occasional moments
for reflection and let God into our shattered life, we will discover
the ability, even the desire, to pray. Our prayer should include a
time of listening—a part of any prayer—to the compassionate
God who is nudging us within, eager to help us find comfort in
the loving divine presence. There we will learn that through our
suffering new life can occur.

If we pray, somewhere along the grief journey a God-
connection will take place. Somewhere along the journey, our
struggle can become a time of intense communication with
God. Somewhere along the journey, the winter in our souls will
begin to melt into spring, a pearl will be formed out of the rough
sand of our sorrow. Somewhere along the journey, the pain of
our loss will turn into healing.

Using This Book

Lift Up Your Hearts is intended to provide meditations—prayer
promptings, if you will—based on the four tasks of grieving.
Parts One through Four, corresponding to the four tasks, each
offer seven Scripture-based meditations to promote reflection
and prayer and thus empower the grief-stricken to experience
the full process of mourning. Because those in mourning tend
to feel the throbs of separation more particularly on anniversaries and holidays, Part Five offers meditations for twelve of
these occasions too. Finally, this book provides annotated
suggested readings, beginning on page 101, as well as prayers,
beginning on page 103, that the bereaved may want to pray.

The meditations in this book do not have to be followed in
any particular order. You can move from meditation to meditation as the Spirit leads you. Spend more time on one and less
on another; or repeat the same one over and over if it nourishes

your languishing spirit. Your mourning is unique to you and so will be the time you take and the method you follow to work through it.

The effort you invest in these meditations can help you become aware of God's loving hands extended in blessing over you. They can make you more sensitive to God's activity in the world at a time when you need it most. Above all, as you meditate on the Scriptures and reflect on your present life, give yourself the opportunity to listen to what God has to say to you. At the beginning of each meditation, take some quiet time to place yourself in God's presence. Breathe in that presence slowly and deeply. Become composed; relax your body; be comfortable in your posture. It is in the quiet of your heart that God's healing grace will be felt. God will be with you on your journey from grief to healing.

The Four Tasks of Grieving

Mourning is each individual's adaptation to the loss of a loved one. There are no rigid step-by-step ways to grieve, no time-tables to keep, no right or wrong ways to begin or end the process. But these are the four fundamental tasks we need to work through after the death of a loved one:

1. To accept the reality of the loss.

Facing the reality of our loss, going through it (there is no going around it), and accepting it as an unchangeable fact is essential for good emotional and physical health, even though it is painful and difficult. It is a process, not a one-time act. The tasks of grieving do not necessarily follow in a specific order, and we may find ourselves returning again and again to come to terms with the fact that the loss has happened. Somehow we need to face, head on, the reality that reunion with our loved one in this world is impossible.

2. To experience the pain of grief.

The pain of separation after a loss is usually a very intense experience, and our feelings at such a time can overwhelm us.

While working through the second task of grieving, it is important to name and face all our emotions, not flee from them. Although we may not be used to expressing these feelings, we can come to understand that they are a part of the mourning process and represent a normal, healthy reaction to grief, as painful as they may be.

3. To adjust to an environment in which the deceased is absent.

The loss of a loved one forever changes our world. We find ourselves in a new environment both personally and socially. An ending has occurred that demands new beginnings. Before this can happen, though, a period of transition has to take place. While working through the third task of mourning, we need to examine closely what has been lost and what has been gained as a consequence of our loss. What experiences, roles, expectations, values, opportunities, and dreams are to be abandoned? What new ones are to be assumed?

4. To emotionally relocate the deceased and move on with life.

Rearranging and re-creating cherished memories of the person who has died is the focus of the fourth task. As we do that we gradually move toward finding a new place in our hearts for our deceased loved one. In time we repossess the energy that we once put into that relationship and reinvest it in our present life and new relationships, even while holding on to our special memories of the one who has died.

Part One

Accepting the Reality

-1-

Not What I Want

Prayer

O God of compassion and tenderness, come to my aid, I pray. I am fragile and in pain. Help me!

Psalm

Hear my prayer, O LORD;
   let my cry come to you. (Psalm 102:1)

Gospel

Then Jesus went with them to a place called Gethsemane.... He took with him Peter and the two sons of Zebedee.... Then he said to them, "I am deeply grieved, even to death; remain here and stay awake with me." And going a little further, he threw himself on the ground and prayed, "My Father, if it is possible, let this cup pass from me; yet not what I want but what you want." (Matthew 26:36–39)

Reflection

How often during the course of my life have I prayed the first part of Jesus' prayer, "Let this cup pass from me"? So many difficult things have happened to me and to those I love. And what has my prayer usually been? "Make my loved one better. Give me more. Make the pain less. Let me be successful. Help me do better. Make the sun rise in my life; don't let it set just yet. Give me what I think I deserve. Don't let me want for anything. Give, Lord, don't take away! Let this cup pass from me!"

Yet, as difficult as my life has been, it is nothing in comparison with the loss I suffer now, the death of my loved one. Did this really happen? Can it be true? Why is my cup of suffering filled to the brim? That is not what I want. Where have you been through all of this, Lord? Why? Why?

And the difficult part is that I have no answers to these questions. Just pain and suffering and dark uncertainty. How hard it is for me to live with all this.

Questions

What do I want to hear from God?

What are the questions that I really need answered?

Closing Prayer

Jesus, the pain you felt in the Garden at the thought of your death caused you to question your Father. My pain has caused me to ask questions too. Help me to ask them, straight from the heart, and then to do as you did, open myself completely to your Father's will.

I Can't Believe This

Prayer

My faith is being tested, O God, my protector. Not understanding, being confused—how much I need to know that you are with me, even if sometimes I see no sign of you in my life. I need your support as never before.

Psalm

Let the words of my mouth and the meditation of my heart
be acceptable to you,
O Lord, my rock and my redeemer. (Psalm 19:14)

Gospel

But Thomas, one of the twelve, was not with them when Jesus came. So the other disciples told him, "We have seen the Lord." But he said to them, "Unless I see the mark of the nails in his hands, and put my finger in the mark of the nails and my hand in his side, I will not believe." (John 20:24-25)

Reflection

Many times when I have to do something I don't want to, or endure something unpleasant, I tend to dream or fantasize that there is no problem, no unpleasant situation. In a way, my fantasy blocks for a time the pain of facing the reality of life.

This is the way it has been for me with the death of my loved one. In a way, I think that denying the fact of death can evade or at least postpone the pain that is inevitable. My denial acts for a time on my ragged emotions like an anesthetic on a wounded body. But I know that, just as anesthesia wears off eventually, I'll have to go through the pain that is part of reality and part of my recuperation.

I had gotten very used to the routines of my loved one; they became familiar and comfortable and gave me a sense of security. Now that they are no more, I find I can sometimes recapture a sense of security by denying the reality of the death.

But I realize that facing and accepting the death is a necessary condition for continuing my own life. That is where my security will eventually lie.

Question

What are some of the routines that will change because of my loved one's death?

Closing Prayer

Help me, Jesus, to begin to face and understand the death of my loved one. It's hard to believe that this has really happened. In fact, I don't even want to believe it. Oh, that I may see and understand. Open my eyes, I pray.

-3-

Where Were You, God?

Prayer

O God, ever present and eager to be with those you love, where are you as I try to pray? I need you, but I cannot feel your presence. Strengthen my faith in my time of trial.

Psalm

Answer me quickly, O Lord;
   my spirit fails.
Do not hide your face from me. (Psalm 143:7)

Gospel

When Jesus arrived, he found that Lazarus had already been in the tomb four days.... When Martha heard that Jesus was coming she went and met him, while Mary stayed at home. Martha said to Jesus, "Lord, if you had been here, my brother would not have died." (John 11:17, 20-21)

Reflection

From childhood I have been taught that God never abandons me, that God is always there for me, and hears my prayer. Yet at this time in my life when I am experiencing the deepest sorrow I have ever encountered, I question God's presence.

"Where were you when my loved one died?" is my question over and over again. "Where was the God who promised to be with me always?" I seem to echo and re-echo Martha's stern admonition: "Lord, if you had been here, my loved one would not have died." That is how I feel. Death came too soon, without warning, without necessity. "Lord, if you had been here..."

I begin to question God's promises, and even my very faith in God. Does this mean I am without faith, without love for the God who is the giver of life? Or am I like Martha who questions, but who can eventually say after listening to her Lord, "I know that my loved one will rise again"?

Question

What is it about God that I want to question at this time?

Closing Prayer

Jesus, help me not only to repeat but to believe your words: "My precious child, I love you and I would not leave you. During your times of trial and suffering, when you see only one set of footprints, it was then that I carried you." ("Footprints," author unknown)

- 4 -

What Happened?

Prayer

O God, bless me with your Spirit to strengthen and console me. Let me be open to all the details of my loved one's passing and find solace in knowing that my loved one was the object of your undying love.

Psalm

Out of the depths I cry to you, O Lord.
    Lord, hear my voice! (Psalm 130:1-2)

Gospel

Soon afterwards he went to a town called Nain, and his disciples and a large crowd went with him. As he approached the gate of the town, a man who had died was being carried out. He was his mother's only son, and she was a widow; and with her was a large crowd from the town. When the Lord saw her, he had compassion for her and said to her, "Do not weep." (Luke 7:11-13)

Reflection

It's so difficult to think about what happened to my loved one. Somehow I felt my loved one would live forever, or at least beyond me. I find myself asking questions: "Why can't we live together forever?" "Why can't we die together?" That would be so much easier.

But what about the death of my loved one? How did all this happen? I need to remember, to be sure of certain things, as much as I can. I have to be able to recount the details so I can pass on my departed one's story to those who care.

This time is for me, to be alone. A time to put together the pieces of my heart that have been broken.

Questions

How did my loved one's death take place?

What did we talk about in our last conversation?

Closing Prayer

Jesus, have compassion on me. There were so many things left unsaid between my loved one and me. Give me the courage, as I mourn this death, to converse with you openly and with loving tenderness about what is in my heart.

-5-

What Was Said?

Prayer

O God, who can read my heart and know my thoughts, you know how I feel. It is so hard for me to pray or to express anything. Help me, then, to be a good listener and to know that you speak to my heart.

Psalm

In my distress I called upon the LORD;
    to my God I cried for help. (Psalm 18:6)

Gospel

Now on that same day two of them were going to a village called Emmaus, about seven miles from Jerusalem, and talking with each other about all these things that had happened. While they were talking and discussing, Jesus himself came near and went with them, but their eyes were kept from recognizing him.... Then one of them, whose name was Cleopas, answered him, "Are you the only stranger in Jerusalem who does not know the things that have taken place there in these days?" (Luke 24:13-16, 18)

Reflection

As I take the time to think about all that has happened, it's important to try to remember what the wake, the funeral, and the burial were like. That was when so many people paid tribute to the one I loved. They told me touching stories at the wake, some of which I had never heard before. In a way, I got to know my loved one even better, because I was seeing that life through others' eyes.

The memorial service was my formal good-bye. The prayers, music, eulogy, and blessings of the ceremony, although wrenching to hear, were a way of acknowledging God's love and blessings, a way of recognizing that God shares with all of us who feel stripped of one of the most splendid blessings of creation, our loved one.

Questions

What was at least one new story that I heard about my loved one at the wake?

What did the priest/minister say about my loved one at the funeral service?

Closing Prayer

Jesus, my loved one touched so many lives in many different ways. I have gotten to know this even more because of the stories I've heard. Bless the storytellers, and bless me as I continue to listen to their stories. Let my heart be open to accept them.

-6-

A Place of Rest

Prayer

O God, my loving parent, you are always with me. Let me find peace and rest in the awareness of your enduring presence and in the assurance that my loved one lives with you forever.

Psalm

To you, O LORD, I call;
    my rock, do not refuse to hear me.
for if you are silent to me,
    I shall be like those who go down to the Pit.

(Psalm 28:1)

Gospel

After these things, Joseph of Arimathea who was a disciple of Jesus asked Pilate to let him take away the body of Jesus.... Nicodemus, who had at first come to Jesus by night, also came, bringing a mixture of myrrh and aloes, weighing about a hundred pounds. They took the body of Jesus and wrapped it with the spices in linen cloths...and the tomb was nearby [so] they laid him there. (John 19:38, 39-41)

Reflection

The cemetery is immense, but quiet and dignified in the ordered rows of headstones, each one identifying someone precious to others. Here is where my loved one's remains were laid to rest. Here is a place I can go to remember, to pray, to cry, where I can place flowers as a token of my undying love. It is a resting place. Perhaps I can find some rest and peace here also.

But to find what I'm looking for, there are some things I'll want to talk over with my loved one, some thoughts or feelings I didn't get a chance to express before death. I know I will have the time to do that now, because I can return again and again to this precious spot where my loved one rests, and converse heart to heart.

Question

What do I want to say to my loved one today?

Closing Prayer

As I visit this resting place, Jesus, help me to share what is in my heart with my loved one. Let me be open and loving, forgiving and caring. Let me always be reverent at this sacred site.

-7-

What Shall I Tell Them?

Prayer

O God of the living, my loved one is no longer with me, except in my memories. I thank you for them. Grant that I may keep the memories of my loved one alive by sharing them with others.

Psalm

O God, do not keep silence;
　do not hold your peace or be still, O God! (Psalm 83:1)

Gospel

He said to them, "Is a lamp brought in to be put under the bushel basket, or under the bed, and not on the lampstand? For there is nothing hidden, except to be disclosed; nor is anything secret, except to come to light. Let anyone with ears to hear listen!" (Mark 4:21-23)

Reflection

There is so much that I need to think about now. My loved one's life was a full one, even though it wasn't as long as I would have liked. And the story of that life, so precious to me, needs to be told so that others will come to know my loved one better.

Who knows that life better than I? I was privileged that the one I loved so dearly also loved me. If the story of that love can be shared with others, then the love can reach beyond the grave and comfort me through life.

I can hardly think right now, because my loved one's death was such a short time ago. But accumulating these treasured memories will keep this love alive and help me move through this painful time. The memories can be a strength to me and to those who reach out to me in affectionate care.

Question

Why was my loved one so very special to me, unequaled in my eyes?

Closing Prayer

Jesus, we are made in the image of God and called to imitate you. Thank you for the reflection of you that I saw in my loved one. Let it remain with me as I struggle through my journey of grief.

Part Two

Experiencing the Pain

-8-

Living the Pain

Prayer

O God of mercy, my pain is so great I can hardly bear it. I call out to you. Hear my prayer and touch my aching spirit.

Psalm

Help me, O LORD my God!
    Save me according to your steadfast love.

(Psalm 109:26)

Gospel

Then Pilate took Jesus and had him flogged. And the soldiers wove a crown of thorns and put it on his head, and they dressed him in a purple robe. They kept coming up to him, saying, "Hail, King of the Jews!" and striking him on the face. (John 19:1-3)

Reflection

I have been separated from the one I love and feel overwhelmed with sadness. My pain is so intense I can feel it physically as well as emotionally. Sometimes I'm almost completely out of control, and I don't know what to do. Many times, because of my grief, I don't understand the feelings inside me.

I keep wondering if I'm normal. There are times when I experience anger and helplessness, guilt and anxiety—all at the same time, never at the right time. I find it difficult to accept these feelings; I don't know if they are right or wrong.

People keep telling me to be strong, not to cry, to keep busy, and not to give in to my feelings. But no matter what they tell me, I know that I am in distress and utterly sad.

I can't pray and sometimes it's hard even to speak. But somehow I realize that I must sort out my feelings and face the anguish of those feelings.

Questions

What feelings do I experience most strongly because of the death of my loved one?

These days, how am I expressing my feelings?

Closing Prayer

Jesus, you felt the unbearable pain of flogging and humiliation. I am physically and emotionally in pain right now. Help me to bear this grief, to face up to it, and to understand the painful emotions that it has caused. Come and touch me in compassion and love.

-9-

If Only...

Prayer

My feelings overcome me, O God of steadfast love, and I cannot pray. Come, be with me in my grief. Let my silence before you rise as prayer. Accept my tears as my prayer in this time of need.

Psalm

Let your steadfast love come to me, O LORD,
  your salvation according to your promise.

(Psalm 119:41)

Gospel

Peter was following at a distance. When they had kindled a fire in the middle of the courtyard and sat down together, Peter sat among them. Then a servant-girl, seeing him in the firelight, stared at him and said, "This man also was with him." But he denied it, saying, "Woman, I do not know him." ...At that moment, while he was still speaking, the cock crowed. The Lord turned and looked at Peter. Then Peter remembered the word of the Lord, how he had said to him, "Before the cock crows today, you will deny me three times." And he went out and wept bitterly. (Luke 22:54-57, 60-62)

Reflection

Like Peter, I find myself at times weeping bitterly. I can imagine what caused him to cry: his denial of Jesus. "If only," I'm sure he was thinking, "I had the courage to tell the world I knew Jesus and loved him."

I'm sure Peter was filled with a lot of "if onlys...." I know I am. If only I had been more perceptive, or more careful, or more insistent, or even more loving. If only I had known that my loved one would die so soon. My "if onlys" cause me the deepest sense of guilt, just as Peter must have felt.

What is this deep-rooted guilt within me? Why do I blame myself for not being more perfect? Who has it all together in every situation? Why can't I just accept myself as human, with the gifts and shortcomings I have?

If I were more virtuous, more this and more that, I probably would have done things differently, perhaps with more sensitivity and understanding. But I am capable only of doing the best I can. The more I give in to this unfounded guilt, the less likely I will be able to move through this grieving process. Somehow I need to face my feelings of guilt and deal with them.

Question

What do I feel guilty about in regard to the death of my loved one?

Closing Prayer

Jesus, help me to face each of my guilty feelings as the human person I am, not as the "perfect one." Let me realize that you so loved us that you were willing to lay down your life for us, that you love us as we are, just as you loved Peter.

-10-

I Don't Deserve This

Prayer

O God of patience, sometimes my anger consumes me. Send your Spirit to enlighten me. Help me to understand why I am so angry, what it means, what I should do with my anger.

Psalm

Rise up, O LORD, O God, lift up your hand;
    do not forget the oppressed. (Psalm 10:12)

Gospel

When Herod saw that he had been tricked by the wise men, he was infuriated, and he sent and killed all the children in and around Bethlehem who were two years old or under, according to the time that he had learned from the wise men. Then was fulfilled what had been spoken through the prophet Jeremiah:

> *"A voice was heard in Ramah,*
> *wailing and loud lamentation,*
> *Rachel weeping for her children;*
> *she refused to be consoled, because*
> *they are no more." (Matthew 2:16-18)*

Reflection

I'm not only crying, but I find myself raging at times. I've never known so much anger, and I don't know what to do with it. I'm not usually a person who gets angry easily, so this persistent feeling is strange to me. I don't like feeling this way. Why has this happened to me? The one I cherished is no more! Like Rachel, I cannot be consoled.

My anger has left me helpless. I look for ways to express how I feel. I know crying has helped, but somehow I need to talk out my anger.

Couldn't the doctors and nurses have tried harder to save my loved one? And what about you, God? Why did you let this happen? What kind of God lets suffering happen? But there are no answers to those questions, are there? And because there are no answers, I find myself angry at you, God. I'm even angry at my loved one because I've been left alone in my agony. Where will this wrath lead me?

Question

How can I constructively deal with my feelings of anger?

Closing Prayer

Jesus, you knew anger. Be with me through my periods of anger. Show me the way to express how I feel. Help me to look at the positive side of things during this dark, trying time in my life.

Unless I See

Prayer

O life-giving God, I still find it hard to believe what has happened. I need an explanation about the "whys" of death. Why was the one I loved taken from me? Grant that I may better understand how death is part of your plan for us.

Psalm

In my distress I cry to the LORD,
   that he may answer me. (Psalm 120:1)

Gospel

But Thomas (who was called the Twin), one of the twelve, was not with them when Jesus came. So the other disciples told him, "We have seen the Lord." But he said to them, "Unless I see the mark of the nails in his hands, and put my finger in the mark of the nails and my hand in his side, I will not believe." (John 20:24-25)

Reflection

I sometimes think if I had been a better person my loved one would not have died. If only I had been more attentive, perhaps more loving and understanding; if only I had had the foresight to appreciate that our time would be so short, that time is always too short.

I even tried to bargain with God. I was willing to make sacrifices, to pray more. I was even willing to give up my own life so that my loved one might live. But I guess you don't bargain with God. We have to live within the world God created, to live and die according to its rules. If only we could be above the natural world, not just a part of it. If only I really understood all this.

Question

What is it concerning my loved one's death that I am finding so difficult to understand?

Closing Prayer

Help me to take one day at a time, Jesus, and to use that day to know you better and trust you more completely. Help me to see that my loved one's death is not because of some divine decree, but because it is part of our human condition and our way to you, as it was yours to your Father.

-12-

Unable to Mourn

Prayer

My God, I am numb and spiritually paralyzed. There are times I can't even cry. I find no peace or consolation in your presence. Comfort me in my despair and lift my spirits.

Psalm

Give ear to my words, O Lord;
    give heed to my sighing.
Listen to the sound of my cry,
    my King and my God,
        for to you I pray. (Psalm 5:1-2)

Gospel

When Judas, his betrayer, saw that Jesus was condemned, he reported and brought back the thirty pieces of silver to the chief priests and the elders. He said, "I have sinned by betraying innocent blood." But they said, "What is that to us? See to it yourself." Throwing down the pieces of silver in the temple, he departed; and he went and hanged himself. (Matthew 27:3-5)

Reflection

It seems like there is nothing left for me, now that the one I cherished has been taken from me. What is the sense of going on? Life is so empty. We shared so much, even to the depths of our souls, and now my loved one cannot hear my words, understand my feelings, or recognize and reciprocate my love.

I are tired of mourning this death. It hurts to mourn; it makes me sad all the time. I'll do anything to escape the pain. So, I plan not to cry, not to think about it. If I don't talk about my loved one any more, perhaps the pain will go away.

I begin to question myself: Was it because I am a bad person that my loved one died? Didn't I show my love enough? Could I have done more, been more, loved more, cared more? Why didn't I treasure more the gift that was given to me? And above all, why was that gift taken from me? Why didn't my life end instead of my loved one's?

It hurts to mourn, yet the depression I find myself in hurts even more.

Questions

What is hindering my working through this period of grief?

What am I finding so hard to face?

Closing Prayer

Jesus, Judas could not believe that he would be forgiven his human frailty. Let me understand that no matter how much I see myself as a failure, you not only forgive me but love me unconditionally, beyond my understanding.

-13-

Stay with Me

Prayer

O God, you can be such a hidden and silent God some-times. I am so lonely after losing my loved one and feel no one is near me, not even you. I pray that I may recognize your presence. Help me to let others into my life; that is how you may show yourself to me.

Psalm

"Come," my heart says, "see his face!"
Your face, LORD, do I seek.
Do not hide your face from me. (Psalm 27:8-9)

Gospel

Then Jesus went with them to a place called Gethsemane; and he said to his disciples, "Sit here while I go over there and pray." ...And going a little farther, he threw himself on the ground and prayed, "My Father, if it is possible, let this cup pass from me; yet not what I want but what you want." Then he came to the disciples and found them sleeping; and he said to Peter, "So could you not stay awake with me one hour?" (Matthew 26:36, 39-40)

Reflection

How afraid I am to be alone at this time! It's not the fear that something will happen to me if I am not surrounded by people, or not being able to handle difficult situations or decisions if there aren't people to call on for advice. It's not even the fear of being by myself. It's the gut feeling that no matter how many people are around, I will continue to be lonely.

I've been lonely before: the first night at camp when I was young; the first day in kindergarten; the beginning of my first job when everyone seemed to know one another, but not me. But I didn't stay lonely for long on those occasions. My loneliness came from the newness of the situations and soon disappeared once familiarity set in.

But this loneliness is different. It's because the death of the one I loved is permanent, and I'm desolate because I can't change that. My loneliness is not a "first" happening, it's a forever happening.

Questions

Since I can't change the permanence of death, what can I do to work through my loneliness?

Who can I call upon to help me?

Closing Prayer

One of your loneliest times, Jesus, was when you felt your apostles didn't care enough to stay awake in the Garden and pray with you. Help me to be open to those who are reaching out to me at this time. Let me realize that just their presence may lift my spirits, that they may have something helpful to share with me.

-14-

Peace of Mind

Prayer

O God of power and gentleness, I find myself restless, anxious, and fearful. I need the peace of soul that you have promised to those who seek you. Be a peacemaker and instill in me, I pray, the peace of soul and mind that I sorely need.

Psalm

Create in me a clean heart, O God,
   and put a new and right spirit within me. (Psalm 51:10)

Gospel

When it was evening on that day, the first day of the week, and the doors of the house where the disciples had met were locked for fear of the Jews, Jesus came and stood among them and said, "Peace be with you." After he said this, he showed them his hands and his side. Then the disciples rejoiced when they saw the Lord. Jesus said to them again, "Peace be with you. As the Father has sent me, so I send you." (John 20:19-21)

Reflection

Right now it's important to remember how many things I was capable of in my life: did well in studies and sports, played an instrument, contributed to the firm I worked for, wrote articles and poems, spoke in public, cooked decent meals, was a loving partner, sister, brother, parent. There were many things I did well and enjoyed doing.

But now with the death of my loved one it's like I can do nothing on my own, especially take care of myself. Will I ever be able to carry on day by day? What if something happens that I can't handle?

The death of my loved one has made me anxious about my own death. If it can happen to the one I loved so much, it can happen to me. When will I die? How? Will someone be there with me?

I know how fearful the apostles were when Jesus died. They probably felt there was nothing they could do on their own, and perhaps they asked the same questions I ask now. But in the midst of all that anxiety and fear Jesus came to them with his gift of peace. That's the gift I need right now.

Question

At this moment what would make me less anxious and more at peace?

Closing Prayer

Jesus, you brought peace to your distressed disciples and comforted them with your presence. Be a peacemaker for me as well in the midst of my suffering and anxiety. Gift me with your peace.

Part Three

Adjusting to Change

-15-

What Should I Do?

Prayer

I am weighed down and weary, gracious and eternal Father, with all the decisions I must make. Gently lift that burden and grant me the wisdom to see what I must do as I go through this difficult period.

Psalm

Let me hear of your steadfast love in the morning,
    for in you I put my trust. (Psalm 143:8)

Gospel

When his mother Mary had been engaged to Joseph, but before they lived together, she was found to be with child from the Holy Spirit. Her husband Joseph, being a righteous man and unwilling to expose her to public disgrace, planned to dismiss her quietly. But just when he had resolved to do this, an angel of the Lord appeared to him in a dream and said, "Joseph, son of David, do not be afraid to take Mary as your wife, for the child conceived in her is from the Holy Spirit...." When Joseph awoke from sleep, he did as the angel of the Lord commanded him. (Matthew 1:18-20, 24)

Reflection

For most of my life I have been in situations when I had to make decisions. In my early years, I usually asked for help because I lacked the experience and didn't have the necessary information. As I got older, I found I could make more balanced judgments and weigh the pros and cons more easily. For the most part I trusted myself to put all the facts together and make prudent decisions.

Now I find I am almost back to those early years. Many times I'm not sure what to do. I hesitate to make even the smallest decisions; I'm afraid I'll judge unwisely and make a foolish mistake. I try asking others what to do, but I become confused because I get different answers.

My loved one's death has made me insecure, lacking in self-confidence. I seem to be caught between not making any decisions and making too many decisions too quickly.

No one could have been more confused than Joseph when he became aware that Mary was "with child" but not married. He had to make a decision that might forever separate him from his love, and he feared he might regret his decision for the rest of his life. He was not sure of himself, but he knew enough to listen to the promptings of God in his heart.

Questions

What decisions do I need to make right away?

What ones can I wait to make?

Closing Prayer

Jesus, in your compassion you gave sight to the blind. Grant me the vision to see what I ought to do. Grace me, too, with the self-confidence I need to make good decisions as I get back on my feet.

-16-

Where Can I Find Healing?

Prayer

O God, above us and within us, look upon me with loving tenderness. I am bent over with the pain from my loss. It never seems to stop. Grant me, I pray, the strength to reach out to you. I know you'll reach out to me.

Psalm

With my whole heart, I cry; answer me, O Lord.

(Psalm 119:145)

Gospel

Now there was a woman who had been suffering from hemorrhages for twelve years; and though she had spent all she had on physicians, no one could cure her. She came up behind [Jesus] and touched the fringe of his clothes, and immediately her hemorrhage stopped. Then Jesus asked, "Who touched me?" When all denied it, Peter said, "Master, the crowds surround you and press in on you." But Jesus said, "Someone touched me; for I noticed that power had gone out from me." When the woman saw that she could not remain hidden, she came trembling. (Luke 8:43-47)

Reflection

It's difficult to remember, but I was once emotionally healthy and whole. Life wasn't perfect, but I was in control and could handle the problems that came my way. I was confident in my ability to judge situations and work out reasonable solutions.

Now, since my loved one has died, it seems I can't do anything right. Somehow my "wholeness" has been drained. My cherished one was an intricate part of my daily life, and that is no longer true; I feel cut in half, inadequate, at a loss.

I yearn to be well again, to resume the life I knew before.

I seem to have few options left and yet there is something I can choose to do. I can, as the woman in the Scripture story, reach out and ask for support. Will I find that difficult? I know I will! Just like the suffering woman, I may tremble at the thought of asking for help. But just reaching out may be a first step toward healing.

Questions

What kind of healing do I feel I need at this time?

Who can I ask to help me?

Closing Prayer

Jesus, you sensed the pain of the woman who was hemorrhaging just by the way she touched you. Help me in my pain to reach out and touch you. Heal me, Lord; heal me.

-17-

Will I Ever Be Joyful Again?

Prayer

O God our parent, you want your children to be happy. Somehow I seem to have lost the serenity and happiness I knew. Too often I see only the dark side of situations. Shine your light on me that I may see what is, and can be, good and joyous in my life.

Psalm

Be merciful to me, O God, be merciful to me,
for in you my soul takes refuge. (Psalm 57:1)

Gospel

As he was setting out on a journey, a man ran up and knelt before him, and asked him, "Good Teacher, what must I do to inherit eternal life?" ...Jesus, looking at him, loved him and said, "You lack one thing; go, sell what you own, and give the money to the poor, and you will have treasure in heaven; then come, follow me." When he heard this, he was shocked and went away grieving, for he had many possessions. (Mark 10:17, 21-22)

Reflection

There was a time when I was a very happy person and could share my ups and even my downs with those I loved. They were my sounding boards, my weather vanes, the source of much of my joy.

But now one of my loved ones has died and I seem, all of a sudden, to be joyless. Life doesn't have the same meaning it used to. I have lost my enthusiasm for it. The one who helped fill my life is no longer part of my life.

Like the rich young man, I feel that God has now asked too much of me. I also go away grieving, for my most prized "possession" has been denied me. Perhaps this is when I need to look into my own heart for the peace and joy that comes from God's presence and from seeking God every day. Jesus, who loves me unconditionally, just as he did the rich young man, is with me. Do I need to look outside myself for happiness? Can I not find my God within me and recapture the same wonderful qualities that I had before this death?

Questions

What was the source of my joy before this death became part of my life?

Though occupied with my utter lack of joyousness, can I consider how I might bring joy to others?

Closing Prayer

Rekindle in me, Jesus, the joy that has been missing during this time of grieving. Let me recognize that you are the source of my happiness. If I can grasp that, there is hope that I can again be a joy-filled disciple.

-18-

Being More Than What I Can Do

Prayer

Throughout my life I've been defined by the roles I've had. O God, who fashioned me uniquely, grant that I may see beyond my roles, those things I can do, into who I am in and of myself. I know that's how you think of me.

Psalm

I call upon you, O LORD, come quickly to me;
give ear to my voice when I call to you. (Psalm 141:1)

Gospel

Meanwhile, standing near the cross of Jesus were his mother, and his mother's sister, Mary the wife of Clopas, and Mary Magdalene. When Jesus saw his mother and the disciple whom he loved standing beside her, he said to his mother, "Woman, here is your son." Then he said to the disciple, "Here is your mother." And from that hour the disciple took her into his own home. (John 19:25-27)

Reflection

I tend so often to judge myself only by the roles I have taken on in life. It's as if I should be defined by what I have done rather than by who I am. I have striven to be the good mother or father or the perfect wife or husband, the caring sister or brother, the selfless friend or companion, the extraordinary executive or computer whiz, the gifted musician or writer. Whatever my accomplishments and roles have been, they are not the measure of who I am!

And when death claimed my loved one, who helped me create those roles, I was left many times not knowing the real me because the roles no longer existed.

I ask myself, "Have I been just a role in someone's life? Am I not more than that? Am I dead to myself and to the world, now that my loved one has died and I can no longer play out the roles that came from that relationship? Am I now less of a person because of that death? How can I become more aware of who I really am in the eyes of God?"

Question

What gifts do I have to offer myself and others, even though I no longer live out some of the roles I once had in my life?

Closing Prayer

Jesus, you saw in your mother a compassion and love that would not cease once you, her son, died. Though she would no longer be mother to you, you gave her to the world as mother. Help me to see beyond my roles and achievements to the person you created me to be.

-19-

New and Difficult Roles

Prayer

My God, creator of the universe, there are many things I don't know how to do, following my dear one's death. Send your Spirit to guide me as I try to adjust to my new way of life; let me see the wisdom of asking others for help.

Psalm

O God, do not be far from me;
O my God, make haste to help me! (Psalm 71:12)

Gospel

He entered Jericho and was passing through it. A man was there named Zacchaeus; he was a chief tax collector and was rich. He was trying to see who Jesus was, but on account of the crowd he could not, because he was short in stature. So he ran ahead and climbed a sycamore tree to see him, because he was going to pass that way. When Jesus came to the place, he looked up and said to him, "Zacchaeus, hurry and come down; for I must stay at your house today." So he hurried down and was happy to welcome him. (Luke 19:1-6)

Reflection

There were other times in life when I had to adjust to new circumstances. I was uncomfortable then too—but not like I am now. This is more than a new venture, like skiing for the first time or starting my own business. The passing of my loved one has changed my life; it's as though my life is just beginning.

Why do I feel this way? Perhaps it's because there will be so many things to do, roles to take on, and circumstances to adjust to that I never experienced before. So many times my loved one was there with me when I had to face new situations. I either received help with them, or I was brave enough to try them because I was doing them for someone else. Now I'm doing them just for me.

This reminds me of Zacchaeus, who was inspired to go beyond himself, to expand his vision of himself; he wanted "to see who Jesus was." Nothing had prepared him for that moment. I imagine he was once content with being the "wealthy tax collector." Soon he would be the recipient of an invitation to house his Lord. This would be an entirely different role for him.

I know I must begin to explore what new roles I will have to take on, now that my loved one is gone. And I'm scared; this is all so new for me!

Question

What kind of help do I need to seek in order to prepare for my new roles, for a new way of living and being?

Closing Prayer

Jesus, you are the way, the truth, and the life. Help me to prepare for the new tasks and situations that I will inevitably face as I live out these days without my loved one. Walk with me, and fill my days with an awareness of your serene presence.

-20-

Consider the Lilies

Prayer

O God of infinite energy, these days when I feel like I can do nothing, every task seems pointless and exhausting. Energize me and guide me as I look for support during this demoralizing time.

Psalm

In your steadfast love hear my voice;
O Lord, in your justice preserve my life."

(Psalm 119:149)

Gospel

"Consider the ravens: they neither sow nor reap, they have neither storehouse nor barn, and yet God feeds them. Of how much more value are you than the birds! And can any of you by worrying add a single hour to your span of life? If then you are not able to do so small a thing as that, why do you worry about the rest? Consider the lilies, how they grow: they neither toil nor spin; yet I tell you, even Solomon in all his glory was not clothed like one of these." (Luke 12:24-28)

Reflection

So often in the past, before this intense sorrow intruded in my life, I was very capable of taking care of myself and even others. I had enjoyed an inner strength that the support of my loved one enhanced. But now this strength has been drained from me. And I constantly ask, "Will I ever be able to stand up on my own two feet again and provide for what I need to sustain my life?"

Jesus urges us not to worry about what we need for our lives. When he tells us to think about the ravens and the lilies, he is telling us to trust that God will provide for us: "Of how much more value are you than the birds!"

I know trying not to worry about what can happen will take careful thought and courageous faith, and right now my thoughts are scattered and my faith tepid. I keep wondering if my deceased loved one can possibly help me as I work at moving through this period of adjustment.

Questions

How can I begin to "consider the lilies": to rely on God for the things I need?

Who can I ask for help with this?

Closing Prayer

You ask much of me, Jesus, during this time of sorrow. Is it the cost of being your disciple? The journey of grieving has left me exhausted physically, emotionally, and spiritually. I feel almost incapable of believing in your assurance that God will provide for me. Instill in me, I pray, a deep spirit of trust.

-21-

New Day Coming

Prayer

It's beginning to sink in, faithful and unchanging God, that an important part of my life is no longer the way it used to be. There is a newness to my life—a new day—that by your grace I am somehow going to have to create. I will remember what has been, but I must build on it for tomorrow. Empower me to do this, I pray.

Psalm

Your steadfast love, O LORD, endures forever.
Do not forsake the work of your hands. (Psalm 138:8)

Gospel

"No one sews a piece of unshrunk cloth on an old cloak, for the patch pulls away from the cloak, and a worse tear is made. Neither is new wine put into old wineskins; otherwise, the skins burst, and the wine is spilled, and the skins are destroyed; but new wine is put into fresh wineskins, and so both are preserved." (Matthew 9:16-17)

Reflection

When I lost my loved one in death, there was a part of me that died also. I soon realized that life would never be as it was. No matter how hard I tried, I could not change the fact that the precious times we shared would return only in my memory.

The pouring of new wine into old wineskins that Jesus talks about in Matthew's Gospel is much like what I've been trying so hard to do. He instructs me that new wine is preserved if it is put into fresh wineskins, not old ones.

A new life has been thrust upon me, but I've been trying to stuff it into my old patterns of living—and it doesn't fit very well. Somehow, if I am to live a new life after my loved one's death, I must become "new" myself and not hold on to the old ways so tightly that my very life itself can burst apart.

I can and should hold on to some of the old life; memories of it are certainly a means of empowering me. But to begin again, new memories must be created and new tasks undertaken; these are to be my provisions as I journey toward healing.

Question

What is holding me back from facing a new life, while I preserve the precious memories of the old?

Closing Prayer

Grant me the courage, Jesus, to face the dawn of a new life after such a loss. You saw how a death could affect people. With you as my companion, help me to rebuild my life; it is in danger of becoming stale and stagnant.

Part Four

Creating Memories and Goals

-22-

How Great Was My Love

Prayer

O God of steadfast love and kindness, you know what my loved one meant to me. I invested a great deal of myself in our relationship. Enlighten me so that I may discover how to continue my life without my loved one beside me.

Psalm

But as for me, my prayer is to you, O LORD.
    At an acceptable time, O God,
       in the abundance of your steadfast love, answer me.
                           (Psalm 69:13)

Gospel

When Mary came where Jesus was and saw him, she knelt at his feet and said to him, "Lord, if you had been here, my brother would not have died." When Jesus saw her weeping, and the Jews who came with her also weeping, he was greatly disturbed in spirit and deeply moved. He said, "Where have you laid him?" They said to him, "Lord, come and see." Jesus began to weep. So the Jews said, "See how he loved him." (John 11:32-36)

Reflection

I put a lot of myself into my relationship with my loved one. I shared my heart and very being with that wonderful person. I now find myself missing my loved one daily, sometimes hourly. That "missing" causes me to be despondent and to weep as Jesus, Martha, and Mary did at Lazarus's death. And although such crying is healthy for me, part of my healing on this journey of grief, I have begun to realize that I want very much to continue my relationship with my loved one in some way.

Since this relationship can no longer be "active" as it once was, I must seek out a way to revive and reinvent my attachment to my loved one so that gradually I can convert my energy into memories that will help us form a new and different relationship, one that can last forever.

Question

What were some unique aspects of my relationship with my loved one?

Closing Prayer

Jesus, you showed your humanity by weeping at the death of your friend. I am human, too, and have wept many tears. Assist me now to move beyond weeping so that the memories of my loved one will help sustain me through life.

-23-

Cherished Memories

Prayer

At times, O gracious God, it is painful to remember the one I loved. Yet I know that now it is only the memories that will sustain me. Grace me with your presence as I begin the process of collecting those memories and treasuring them.

Psalm

On the day I called you answered me,
  you increased my strength of soul. (Psalm 138:3)

Gospel

Then he took a cup, and after giving thanks he said, "Take this and divide it among yourselves; for I tell you that from now on I will not drink of the fruit of the vine until the kingdom of God comes." Then he took a loaf of bread, and when he had given thanks, he broke it and gave it to them, saying, "This is my body, which is given for you. Do this in remembrance of me." (Luke 22:17-19)

Reflection

Why is it that when I begin to remember, the pain of having lost my loved one seems almost unbearable? Is it because the remembrance includes negative as well as positive aspects of our relationship? Because I am afraid of losing some of the reminiscences I once held so dear? Or is it because I realize that in the remembering I have already been forced to "relocate" that dear person in my emotions? Whatever the reason, I know almost intuitively that memories will at some time have to be assembled and stored.

Although our relationship can no longer be the same as it was, I need to begin to cherish my memories of it. At the Last Supper, Jesus wanted his disciples to remember him forever, and so he gave them a task to perform over and over again, in the breaking of the bread. To remember my loved one forever, I, too, have a task to perform, no matter how disturbing it may be. I need to loosen the bonds of my attachment to my loved one in order to form a new and ongoing relationship with my loved one that no other relationship can erase or diminish.

Question

What "cherishable memories" of my loved one do I want to hold on to for the rest of my life?

Closing Prayer

For two thousand years, Jesus, we have remembered you through the ritual you gave us. With your guidance and support, may I begin to accumulate and store memories about my loved one that I can cherish— memories that will last all the days of my life.

-24-

Memories to Share

Prayer

O my God, you are love itself. There are many stories about my departed one that are stored in my mind and heart, stories I want to share with others I love. By your grace, enable me to recount these stories with love and admiration. Your presence will make it fruitful.

Psalm

I lift up my eyes to the hills—
   from where will my help come? (Psalm 121:1)

Gospel

In those days Mary set out and went with haste to a Judean town in the hill country, where she entered the house of Zechariah and greeted Elizabeth. When Elizabeth heard Mary's greeting, the child leaped in her womb. And Elizabeth was filled with the Holy Spirit and exclaimed with a loud cry, "Blessed are you among women, and blessed is the fruit of your womb. And why has this happened to me, that the mother of my Lord comes to me?" (Luke 1:39-43)

Reflection

When my loved one passed away, I doubted that I'd ever hear that precious name spoken again. I thought people would hesitate to mention it because they believed it would sadden me. But I soon learned, especially at the wake and at the memorial service, that people were eager to share their remembrances. And so, as people shared their stories, we were all comforted by the recollections; my loved one became present to me and to them in the telling.

But now, some time after the services, I find others have become silent on the subject, less inclined to talk about it. Perhaps now they are afraid the remembrance will pain me too much. And because I miss the stories and the continued mention of my loved one's name, not only do I have to collect my own remembrances but I need somehow to share them with others.

Mary must have faced that same desire when she undertook her journey to her cousin Elizabeth. Like Mary, I must not keep my prized memories to myself. By sharing them I will begin to experience a healing process that eventually will lead me to form a new relationship with my dear deceased, a relationship that will be with me forever.

Questions

Who will be the "Elizabeths" in my life?

How will I share my cherished memories with them?

Closing Prayer

Jesus, accompany me as I begin my journey into "the hill country" to share my memories of my loved one. Keep me on that path, and through your Spirit invigorate me to seek out those who will listen to me and share their recollections.

-25-

Needing God

Prayer

Ever-present God, though I sometimes feel angry and want to blame you for the death of my loved one, I am becoming increasingly aware that I need you in my life right now. Allow me to reach out to you as a trusting child.

Psalm

To you, O Lord, I lift up my soul.
O my God, in you I trust. (Psalm 25:1)

Gospel

One of the criminals who were hanged there kept deriding him and saying, "Are you not the Messiah? Save yourself and us!" But the other rebuked him, saying, "Do you not fear God, since you are under the same sentence of condemnation? And we indeed have been condemned justly, for we are getting what we deserve for our deeds, but this man has done nothing wrong." Then he said, "Jesus, remember me when you come into your kingdom." He replied, "Truly I tell you, today you will be with me in Paradise." (Luke 23:39-43)

Reflection

For quite some time now I have found it very difficult to turn to God. The death of my loved one has made me suffer. Sometimes I blame God for the death and the anguish; sometimes I blame others or even myself. And a good deal of the time I want to be left alone with my pain, convinced that nothing can help me.

But I ask myself, "Is this what people do when they are in pain like this? Do they hide from others, or do they seek out those who can help them to heal the wounds and lessen the pain?"

I look at the two criminals who were crucified with Jesus. Both of them were in dreadful pain. One taunted him, seeking only his own benefit, and turned away from Jesus; with trust, the other reached out in humble prayer and shared his pain and contrition with Jesus.

I can take on the attitude of either criminal. No one would deny that the death of my loved one has wounded me. But there is nothing to prevent me from reaching out in faith to Jesus, who also knew pain and loss, asking him to soothe my wounds so I may also gain some semblance of peace. The decision to reach out or not is mine alone.

Question

What hinders me from continually reaching out to God in my need?

Closing Prayer

Listen, Jesus, to my cry in this period of pain. You promised Paradise to the criminal who reached out to you. I know that when I do the same with a trusting heart, you will be there for me.

-26-

Reaching Out

Prayer

O healing God, I have a need right now for others who will help bandage my wounds. Grant me the discernment, humility, and openness to allow others to minister to me. I know that when they come in love, you also come.

Psalm

Hear my prayer, O LORD;
> give ear to my supplication in your faithfulness;
> answer me in your righteousness. (Psalm 143:1)

Gospel

Jesus replied, "A man was going down from Jerusalem to Jericho; and fell into the hands of robbers, who stripped him, beat him, and went away, leaving him half dead.... But a Samaritan while traveling came near him; and when he saw him, he was moved with pity. He went to him and bandaged his wounds, having poured oil and wine on them. Then he put him on his own animal, brought him to an inn, and took care of him." (Luke 10:30, 33-34)

Reflection

Why do I find it so difficult to ask for help? Have I become so independent that I feel I can do everything myself? That may be true in some circumstances, but in the deep sorrow I experience now I am beginning to realize that I can't continue to travel this burdensome journey alone.

The stranger in the gospel story who was beaten, stripped of everything, and left for dead could hardly help himself, but perhaps he reached out feebly to a passer-by. The Samaritan saw the man's pain and helplessness and went to his aid, caring enough to "bandage his wounds" and bring him to an inn.

There are many mourners traveling the road I'm on. Some of them have started out ahead of me; some are struggling behind me. But all appreciate my pain and know what the grieving process is, because they have experienced it themselves.

I must begin "reaching out" to Good Samaritans who might help, people of compassion who know this road well. When I acknowledge that I need help and take steps to get it, then healing can take place. But am I ready at this time to extend myself, to reach beyond myself and seek those who can bandage my wounds?

Question

What will it take for me to ask for help or to offer it to others who are traveling this road of mourning?

Closing Prayer

Instill in me, Jesus, the spirit of humility to recognize my need for others at this time of grieving, and common sense to see that I shouldn't try to make the journey alone. I pray also that I may be conscious of the pain of separation in my fellow travelers.

-27-

Surrounded by Love

Prayer

O God, my father and mother, let me not, through silly pride, think I can undergo all this by myself. I need the support and the compassionate understanding both you and my friends and family offer me.

Psalm

O God, you are my God, I seek you,
   my soul thirsts for you. (Psalm 63:1)

Gospel

People were bringing little children to him in order that he might touch them; and the disciples spoke sternly to them. But when Jesus saw this, he was indignant and said to them, "Let the little children come to me; do not stop them; for it is to such as these that the kingdom of God belongs. Truly I tell you, whoever does not receive the kingdom of God as a little child will never enter it." And he took them up in his arms, laid his hands on them, and blessed them. (Mark 10:13-16)

Reflection

At the time I lost my loved one I was surrounded by people who loved me. Many were aware of my spiritual needs as they performed the religious ceremonies and rituals to help lay my loved one to rest. They later visited me.

Neighbors and friends attended to my physical needs at the time of the death and for some time afterward. I had plenty of offers of food, companionship, transportation, and other helpful services.

Those who reached out in this way supported me emotionally during an unstable time. But now the first days and weeks of grieving have passed, I find myself still in need of support. I have a great yearning to approach Jesus, as the little children did in the gospel story, and be comforted, understood, and cared for.

I know I will also need others to support me in ways I haven't even thought of yet, people who will continue to walk with me on this mournful journey.

Questions

Who will I reach out to at this time to find support?

What kind of support do I need?

Closing Prayer

Jesus, you took the "little children in your arms, laid your hands on them, and blessed them." You insisted that no one should prevent them from approaching you. Open your arms to me now. Lay your healing hands on me. Bless me with your love. Let nothing stop me from drawing near to you.

-28-

Climbing the Mountain

Prayer

O God of wisdom, I need to begin setting goals for myself so that I may move into the future carefully but confidently. Grant me the gifts of insight and courage for this difficult task.

Psalm

O Lord my God, I cried to you for help,
 and you have healed me. (Psalm 30:2)

Gospel

Now the eleven disciples went to Galilee, to the mountain to which Jesus had directed them. When they saw him, they worshiped him; but some doubted. And Jesus came and said to them, "All authority in heaven and on earth has been given to me. Go therefore and make disciples of all nations, baptizing them in the name of the Father and of the Son and of the Holy Spirit, and teaching them to obey everything that I have commanded you. And remember, I am with you always, to the end of the age." (Matthew 28:16-20)

Reflection

There have been so many times during this period of mourning that I felt I would never make it up the mountain of my sorrow. There have been sheer cliffs and crevices along the way, and the path has been steep and sometimes perilous.

But God has summoned me to make this very difficult ascent, leading me just as Jesus directed his disciples to the mountain. It was at the mountaintop, after all, that Jesus gave them their goals for the future of the community of believers, the church. Perhaps it will be at the peak of my mountain that I will begin to envision the goals for my future.

Realistically, I have to set short-term goals first, confident that they are well organized, clear, specific, achievable. Will these goals be life-giving and worth the struggle that inevitably will be mine? Will they help me set off on a new life-journey, even while holding on to my cherished memories? I'll never know the answers to those questions until I am able to assert, "I shall climb the mountain of my grief."

Question

What do I need in my life right now to help me achieve my goals?

Closing Prayer

Jesus, the mountain of my grief sometimes appears too steep to climb. Stir up my courage, I pray; let me be ever mindful that when you sent your disciples to perform difficult tasks you promised them your abiding presence: "I am with you always, to the end of the age." Make that same promise to me!

Part Five

Anniversaries and Holidays

And They Rejoiced

Anniversary of the Day of Birth

Prayer

O God of joy and gladness, births are such wondrous events. I want to celebrate them, but I'm still mourning a life that has ended on this earth. I implore you to arouse my courage so that I may come to terms with this.

Psalm

Make a joyful noise to the LORD, all the earth.
  Worship the LORD with gladness;
    come into his presence with singing. (Psalm 100:1-2)

Gospel

"Do not be afraid, Zechariah, for your prayer has been heard. Your wife Elizabeth will bear you a son, and you will name him John. You will have joy and gladness, and many will rejoice at his birth, for he will be great in the sight of the Lord." (Luke 1:13-15)

Reflection

Birthdays are very special occasions, celebrated with festivity, with singing, cards, food, and gifts. After all, they mark the day on which our family members and friends came into the world and graced our lives.

I've spent many of these occasions rejoicing in the birth of my loved one. I marked my calendar, bought the "goodies," invited guests, and prepared a suitable party at just the right time and place. But now with my loved one gone, I hesitate celebrating that birthday because a life that began in joy has now ended in deep sorrow for me. It's painful to recall the day!

Zechariah and Elizabeth rejoiced at the prospect of their son's birthday. An almost impossible dream, to them, was turned into joyous reality. And a signal feature of his birth was the promise the angel made: "...he will be great in the sight of the Lord."

I am not concerned whether my loved one was "great in the sight of the Lord;" I leave that to God. I know, though, that my loved one's presence was a singular blessing for me. Instead of fleeing the remembrance of my dear one's birth into the world, I should celebrate the day with gratitude.

Question

What am I doing to prepare to celebrate this anniversary of my loved one's birth?

Closing Prayer

Jesus, your cousin John, the one called to prepare for your coming, was greeted at his birth with great joy and love. Enable me to continue to celebrate the birth of my loved one, who spent a lifetime preparing to enjoy your eternal presence.

-30-

A Day to Remember
Anniversary of the Day of Death

Prayer

Ever-living God and Lord of life, the anniversary of my loved one's death is near. I'm torn between trying to forget what happened that day and wanting to remember every precious moment. Enlighten me, I implore you, to appreciate what a meaningful day this can be.

Psalm

Surely goodness and mercy shall follow me
    all the days of my life. (Psalm 23:6)

Gospel

A leader of the synagogue came in and knelt before him, saying, "My daughter has just died; but come and lay your hand on her and she will live." ...When Jesus came to the leader's house and saw the flute players and the crowd making a commotion, he said, "Go away; for the girl is not dead but sleeping." ...But when the crowd had been put outside, he went in and took her by the hand, and the girl got up. (Matthew 9:18, 23-25)

Reflection

Anniversaries may bring pleasant memories, but they also bring remembrances that are melancholy and cause heartache. The anniversary of my loved one's death has its full share, at first, of sadness and disbelief, the attitude that "I still can't believe it happened." I dread the day, yet at the same time something inside urges me to commemorate it in a special way.

The synagogue leader in the gospel episode had just experienced the death of his daughter. "My daughter has just died," he tells Jesus. And I can imagine—because I experienced it myself—what a heart-wrenching day that was for him. But the leader goes on to say, "but come and lay your hand on her and she will live." Could I have said that on the day my dear one died?

My loved one did die, and now I'm approaching the anniversary of the day. What will it be like for me? Should I fear its arrival? Will I spend it in dejection, shut away from any who wish to extend a hand to me? Or will I try to capture the memories that will make me grateful for what I had and aware that my loved one still lives, even now in heaven!

Questions

How can I celebrate my loved one on the anniversary day of death?

Who will I celebrate with?

Closing Prayer

You were compassionate, Jesus, whenever you encountered people in pain or in need of healing. Be tender and gracious to me now, in my pain, as the anniversary of the death of my loved one approaches. Say to me, "Take heart; I am with you."

-31-

Beginning All Over
New Year's Day

Prayer

O God, ever the same and ever new, I am faced with the beginning of a new year. I am afraid of what it may bring. The past has been painful and lonely. By your grace, let me live this coming year in an upbeat and positive way.

Psalm

O sing to the LORD a new song;
    sing to the LORD, all the earth. (Psalm 96:1)

Gospel

Then the son said to him, "Father, I have sinned against heaven and before you; I am no longer worthy to be called your son." But the father said to his slaves, "Quickly, bring out a robe—the best one—and put it on him; put a ring on his finger and sandals on his feet. And get the fatted calf and kill it, and let us eat and celebrate; for this son of mine was dead and is alive again; he was lost and is found!" And they began to celebrate. (Luke 15:21-24)

Reflection

Beginnings are very difficult for me, especially now that my loved one has died. I don't want to "begin again"—all alone. The past that I had shared with my loved one is no more, and the present is filled with sadness, pain, and sometimes even an emotional emptiness. It's almost as if the present is no more.

And now I am prodded to face the future with the start of a new year. I'm not optimistic about what the future holds for me, and that frightens me. But when I reflect on the story concerning the son who left the security of his family and home to find something "more exciting," I'm struck by what he finally discovered: He really needed to return to those who loved him and start all over in a renewed relationship. What he actually encountered on his return was much better than what he ever anticipated, wasn't it? He was anxious about being open to the future, but he took the step that would lead him to a new life with a new attitude. Can I learn from his experience?

Questions

Who will I ask to be there for me as I face the coming year?

In what concrete ways can they help me?

Closing Prayer

I have no idea, Jesus, what this new year will bring; I'm uneasy and troubled about it. Increase my trust in your unreserved love, and enable me to face it—embrace it—in a positive way. Let me be open to the gift that you hold out to me.

-32-

My Undying Love
Valentine's Day

Prayer

Great and loving God, it appears the entire world celebrates "love" on St. Valentine's Day. I've lost my love in death, and I'm having a difficult time with the thought of celebrating this day—or any other day—for that matter. Grant me the grace to understand what love really is.

Psalm

For the word of the LORD is upright,
    and all his work is done in faithfulness.
He loves righteousness and justice;
    the earth is full of the steadfast love of the LORD.

(Psalm 33:4-5)

Gospel

When Jesus saw his mother and the disciple whom he loved standing beside her, he said to his mother, "Women, here is your son." Then he said to the disciple, "Here is your mother." And from that hour the disciple took her into his own home. (John 19:26-27)

Reflection

For many years on this day I expressed my love in verses and song and big red hearts, in affectionate remembrances and embraces. I've not been alone in this; anyone who has ever experienced love seems to crowd all his or her sentiments into Valentine's Day.

But what do I do now without my loved one? How do I move through this day surrounded by celebrations of love and romantic demonstrations, when I feel I have very little to celebrate any more?

Perhaps I can reflect prayerfully on the gospel scene that celebrates love at its greatest. In his all-embracing, dying act of love, Jesus shares his mother with us, through his beloved apostle, John. What great love for us Jesus expresses in this extraordinary act of giving.

This is the kind of love that is worth celebrating: thoughtful, unselfish, committed, faithful. If this is the kind of love my cherished one and I shared, it is eminently worth celebrating. Death cannot cause it to die. I will remember it and celebrate it all my days.

Question

How can I begin to celebrate with others the love I have shared with my loved one?

Closing Prayer

Jesus, you taught us about love and demonstrated it in everyday living. Teach me more about love, I pray, and keep my heart open in affectionate remembrance of my dear one who died. Open my heart as well to those I come upon each day.

-33-

Into Your Hands
Good Friday

Prayer

Dying and death are so hard to understand, O heavenly God. If only I could be sure that my loved one is safe and happy. Increase my faith in the life you have prepared for us after our time on earth. I commend my loved one into your hands.

Psalm

Insults have broken my heart,
    so that I am in despair.
I looked for pity, but there was none;
    and for comforters, but I found none. (Palm 69:20)

Gospel

It was now about noon, and darkness came over the whole land until three in the afternoon, while the sun's light failed; and the curtain of the temple was torn in two. Then Jesus, crying with a loud voice, said "Father, into your hands I commend my spirit." Having said this, he breathed his last. (Luke 23:44-46)

Reflection

As I commemorate the death of Jesus today, I can imagine what a sad day it was for those who loved him, because I still find it difficult to handle the passing of my own loved one. "Gone forever," I keep saying to myself. And with that, I ask, "Gone where?" My response? "Gone to be with God, forever."

I'm sure Mary and those who stood with her at the cross also wondered about Jesus after his death. They weren't even sure where they would bury his body. They had heard Jesus speak of rising, but it was still before the resurrection, after all. On the cross, Jesus clarified what would ultimately happen to him after his death: "Father, into your hands I commend my spirit." He would return to his Father, who had sent him to us, as one of us.

I want so much to commend my loved one into God's hands. There the one I have loved will find comfort and complete fulfillment. If this is where Jesus our brother made his eternal dwelling place, my loved one can too.

Questions

What is standing in the way of my believing that my loved one is in God's hands?

How am I going to resolve these obstacles?

Closing Prayer

Comfort me, Jesus, as you did those who stood by you at the cross. You placed yourself in your Father's hands, showing us what we are to do at our death and reminding us of our destiny, which is to be taken into God's embrace. Let me find comfort, Jesus, in the certain knowledge that my loved one is now resting in the presence of your Father in heaven.

-34-

Hope for New Life
Easter

Prayer

Your son's life and death, ever-living God, led to this feast that celebrates and ensures new and eternal life. I pray for that life for my dear departed one. Help me to absorb the message conveyed to the women at the tomb: "He is not here, but has risen."

Psalm

How lovely is your dwelling place,
O LORD of hosts!
My soul longs, indeed it faints
for the courts of the LORD. (Psalm 84:1-2)

Gospel

They found the stone rolled away from the tomb, but when they went in, they did not find the body. While they were perplexed about this, suddenly two men in dazzling clothes stood before them. The women were terrified, and bowed their faces to the ground, but the men said to them, "Why do you look for the living among the dead? He is not here, but has risen!" (Luke 24:2-5)

Reflection

Even though the Easter season is supposed to be a time of jubilant celebration, even though spring is beginning to blossom into bright colors and signs of new life, I still feel the heavy sadness of losing the one I loved so dearly. It's hard to celebrate or even to enter another season without my loved one. All life seems gone from me, and yet nature and the church proclaims that new life is about to happen.

I need to consider what the church celebrates today: new life springing from death. How sad the women were at Jesus' tomb, but they heard the good news, "He is not here, but has risen." Have I heard that same message without really believing it?

New life rises from death. The same message is repeated in countless ways each spring in nature. Why can't I accept that my loved one's death was not the end? Jesus' life was not taken away, only changed. I have God's word for it: My loved one lives! Can I bring Easter joy to this realization?

Question

What do I need to do to better understand and accept the fact that from death comes new life?

Closing Prayer

Jesus, because of your death and resurrection I believe that my life and my loved one's are eternal, that death has no sting, no victory. In my moments of loneliness and despondence, let that belief raise my spirits.

-35-

Forever Remembered
Memorial Day

Prayer

My God, I pray that this day of remembering all of our loved ones' deaths may stir my faith in you, with whom my departed one lives. Let that faith encourage and sustain me during these trying times.

Psalm

O send out your light and your truth;
    let them lead me;
let them bring me to your holy hill
    and to your dwelling. (Psalm 43:3)

Gospel

Jesus went with them, but when he was not far from the house, the centurion sent friends to say to him, "Lord, do not trouble yourself, for I am not worthy to have you come under my roof; therefore I did not presume to come to you. But only speak the word, and let my servant be healed." When Jesus heard this he was amazed at him, and turning to the crowd that followed him, he said, "I tell you, not even in Israel have I found such faith." (Luke 7:2-3, 6-7, 9)

Reflection

The nation celebrates Memorial Day and salutes those who gave up their lives in defense of our country. We memorialize them with parades and parties, fireworks and church services. We remember them in prayer and story, articles and songs, honoring their heroism.

How can I "memorialize" my loved one, not in parades or parties, but in my heart? Is there a way that my memories may help me live more fully and joyfully now and in the future?

One way is to continue (or even begin) to gather memories of my loved one and store them in my heart. I want to pass on the story of a life that meant so much to me. I can memorialize this life in spoken and written word. I know there are many who want to hear it.

The centurion in the gospel had so much faith that he asked Jesus just to "speak" and his servant would be cured. Perhaps if I speak or write out my memories, healing will take place in me. I need to celebrate my memories and one day be healed.

Question

What are the most important memories I want to share with those who knew my loved one?

Closing Prayer

Jesus, you rewarded the centurion's faith by restoring his servant to health. Send your Spirit, the comforter, upon me that I may find inner healing. I put my faith and trust in you.

-36-

Freedom to Grow
Independence Day

Prayer

My God, Lord of the world, be Lord of my heart. You have graced me with the capacity to grow after my loved one's death. But I feel so listless, without ambition. Guide me in the coming months to assert myself emotionally, socially, and spiritually, so that I live in a way that pleases you.

Psalm

I waited patiently for the LORD;
    he inclined to me and heard my cry.
He drew me up from the desolate pit,
    out of the miry bog. (Psalm 40:1-2)

Gospel

On the third day there was a wedding in Cana of Galilee, and the mother of Jesus was there. Jesus and his disciples had also been invited to the wedding. When the wine gave out, the mother of Jesus said to him, "They have no wine." And Jesus said to her, "Woman, what concern is that to you and to me? My hour has not yet come." His mother said to the servants, "Do whatever he tells you." (John 2:1-5)

Reflection

The freedom to make decisions for myself is a priceless gift. Independence Day celebrates our forebears' conscious decision to liberate themselves from oppression. That one decision led to the beginning of our country's remarkable development.

I'm fearful of the freedom involved in making a commitment to grow myself without the presence and help of my loved one. But I can't remain fearful. It isn't healthy for me, and I know my loved one would not want me to be afraid.

At the wedding feast at Cana, Mary overcame her fear of making a mistake. She insisted that Jesus do something to help others, even if he felt he was not ready. I must do the same.

I recognize that the decision to grow is mine alone. Can I afford not to take the chance?

Question

What will it take for me to risk struggling to use my freedom to develop as I should?

Closing Prayer

Jesus, your mother used her free will and courage to urge you to begin your ministry. Help me to see my unwanted "independence" from my loved one as an opportunity to fight for the development of my own life that I so desperately need.

-37-

Moving On
Labor Day

Prayer

O indwelling God, I can no longer stand still. I must, in spite of my loss, move beyond this period of grieving and get on with my life. Touch my spirit with the courage and energy to work through this difficult time. Whatever the future holds for me, I know you will be at my side.

Psalm

Unless the LORD build the house,
  those who build it labor in vain. (Psalm 127:1)

Gospel

A woman in the city, who was a sinner, having learned that he was eating in the Pharisee's house, brought an alabaster jar of ointment. She stood behind him at his feet, weeping, and began to bathe his feet with her tears and to dry them with her hair. Then she continued kissing his feet and anointing them with the ointment. Now when the Pharisee who had invited him saw it, he said to himself, "If this man were a prophet, he would have known who and what kind of woman this is who is touching him—that she is a sinner." Jesus spoke up and said to him, "…I tell you, her sins, which were many, have been forgiven; hence she has shown great love. But the one to whom little is forgiven, loves little." (Luke 7:37-40, 47)

Reflection

I don't look forward to summer's end. As hard as the season has been for me, at least the days were sunny and warm and bright with life. But this holiday in September reminds me that days will become shorter, perhaps cold, certainly dreary. And I ask myself how I will get through the months ahead.

What am I afraid of? I've lived through the worst of times with the loss of my loved one. What could be harder? And yet as I ask that, I know that the work required to move on with my life may indeed become harder. Harder because I will have to change!

I ponder the story about the sinful woman who changed her life in a single incident, a meaningful act of devotion. As a woman who wasn't accepted or even tolerated, she had to work hard at turning her life around and moving on with it. But in reaching out to Jesus, in working through her weaknesses, she received the help she needed. What she brought to the incident was her love; what she received was forgiveness, encouragement, and guidance. I wonder if I possess the same degree of love and determination!

Question

What is hindering me from the hard work that it will take to move on with my life?

Closing Prayer

Jesus, you helped the sinful woman change the course of her life because she reached out to you in love and you rewarded her faith with your blessing. Grant that I may mirror her courage as I strive to move on in life. Remind me often that you and others love me. That will give me the fortitude I need to work my way through my grief.

-38-

We Are Blessed
All Saints Day/All Souls Day

Prayer

O saving God, I believe my loved one is with you in heaven. Let me find consolation in that thought. How wonderful it is to have my own saint in heaven.

Psalm

Even the sparrow finds a home,
   and the swallow a nest for herself,
   where she may lay her young,
at your altars, O LORD of hosts,
   my King and my God.
Happy are those who live in your house,
   ever singing your praise. (Psalm 84:3-4)

Gospel

Then [Jesus] began to speak, and taught them, saying:
   "Blessed are the poor in spirit, for theirs is the kingdom of heaven.
   "Blessed are those who mourn, for they shall be comforted." (Matthew 5:2-4)

Reflection

What does it mean to be blessed? Sanctified by God? Content? Distinguished in love? Joyous? I know that the saints in heaven are all this and whatever else God has prepared for those who love God.

Today I celebrate with the church the blessedness of those of God's family who now enjoy unending life with God. My departed one lived a good life; happiness and love characterized it. Why can't "eternal life" for my loved one be an extension of that life?

I believe that God is faithful, keeping the promises made to us. Being poor in spirit, hungry for justice, pure in heart, a peacemaker, merciful—these are the things Jesus demanded of his disciples, then and today. My loved one lived the beatitudes. It is important for me to believe that the promised reward has been gained.

Question

What does it mean to me, as I live out the rest of my life, that my loved one now enjoys the happiness of heaven?

Closing Prayer

In the beatitudes, Jesus, you described what your faithful disciples may expect to receive for living in a way worthy of the "communion of saints." My loved one now enjoys the reward you promised. Help me to live the beatitudes so that at the end of my life I, too, can be one of the blessed, with you and all the saints.

-39-

Being Grateful
Thanksgiving

Prayer

O God, maker of all that is good, it's so hard to be thankful for anything since my loved one died. My greatest gift is gone. Am I to thank you for that? What do I have to be grateful for as the rest of the world celebrates this Thanksgiving Day? In spite of this biting complaint, let me hold out my hand to you in faith.

Psalm

O give thanks to the LORD, for he is good,
    for his steadfast love endures forever.
O give thanks to the God of gods,
    for his steadfast love endures forever. (Psalm 136:1-2)

Gospel

As [Jesus] entered a village, ten lepers approached him. Keeping their distance, they called out, saying, "Jesus, Master, have mercy on us!" When he saw them, he said to them, "Go and show yourselves to the priests." And as they went, they were made clean. Then one of them, when he saw that he was healed, turned back, praising God with a loud voice. He prostrated himself at Jesus' feet and thanked him. (Luke 17:12-16)

Reflection

Unlike earlier times, I now dread the approach of Thanksgiving Day. I keep asking myself what there is to be thankful for, considering the death of my loved one. This Thanksgiving will be so different. Even though my family will all be seated around the table to continue the tradition started long ago, one setting will be empty, at least in my mind. What I was once most grateful for is no longer with me.

The ten lepers in the gospel story were healed of their infirmity. I've never understood how ten received such a miracle and only one could say thanks. It would have been so easy for all of them to thank Jesus for making them "clean."

As I think about that, I wonder if perhaps I am like the nine who could have expressed gratitude to Jesus, but did not. My loved one has died, and I certainly don't feel thankful for that. But have I forgotten so soon to give thanks for the loving relationship we had that meant more to me than life itself?

I need to let the celebration of Thanksgiving Day be a reminder that God gifted me with someone I loved and who loved me. That is truly something to be deeply grateful for.

Questions

How can I celebrate and give thanks for the gift of love I have received?

In what particular way could I show my gratitude to God and others this Thanksgiving Day?

Closing Prayer

Jesus, the greatest gift you gave the lepers was healing them of the heavy burden they carried. Relieve me of the sorrow I carry from the death of my loved one. Open my eyes to see beyond the sadness and to realize that I am indebted to you for the gift of love you have given me.

-40-

Mixed Feelings
Christmas

Prayer

O God, father of Jesus and my father, it's Christmas time and all around me people are celebrating. I feel envious. It's hard to bring myself to any level of celebration. Since the death of my dear one, I often feel unenthusiastic, sluggish. Stir up in me, God, the spark of new life, a renewed excitement about life.

Psalm

You have turned my mourning into dancing;
    you have taken off my sackcloth
    and clothed me with joy. (Psalm 30:11)

Gospel

[Joseph] went to be registered with Mary, to whom he was engaged and who was expecting a child. While they were there, the time came for her to deliver her child. And she gave birth to her firstborn son and wrapped him in bands of cloth, and laid him in a manger, because there was no place for them in the inn. (Luke 2:5-7)

Reflection

This seems to be such a happy time for people, so many things going on in celebration of Christmas. You can't go anywhere without being reminded of "joy to the world," or "all is calm, all is bright," or mistletoe, or sleigh bells and snow, or an infant in a feed trough who would be called Messiah and Savior. I have mixed feelings during this season. I don't feel calm or bright or joyful—I feel lonely—but how can I escape what is going on around me? Or should I escape it?

Then I think about the story of Jesus' birth. There certainly was reason for happiness: Jesus was born, and the angels proclaimed the good news, shepherds rejoiced at the manger, and stars shone brightly. But amid all the gladness there was also reason for concern. Jesus' parents had nowhere to lay him down except in a stable. No warm blanket, no little cap for his head, just "bands of cloth" to put around him. They certainly must have had mixed feelings concerning the sacred event that first Christmas.

I won't really get into the spirit of the Christmas season this year. I need time to be quiet and reflective, to sort out my feelings and memories. And perhaps I should be content with the fact that my mixed feelings are just a mirror of what life is like; it is not always upbeat, but it is not always somber and beset with problems, either.

Question

What can I do, without being disrespectful of my loved one's memory, to find my way through this Christmas season with a little joy?

Closing Prayer

Jesus, you are Immanuel, God with us. In your loving kindness, be with me as I struggle through this Christmas season. You know the emptiness I feel. Guide me to find the new life that your birth signaled to the world.

Further Reading

When Bad Things Happen to Good People, Harold S. Kushner, Avon Books, 1981. This book is written for those who have suffered because of the illness or death of another, or because of rejection and despair; it is for those seeking a loving and just God in our unjust world.

Heart Peace: Healing Help for Grieving Folks, Richard Gilbert, Abbey Press, 1996. This book leads us in a gentle way through the process of grieving. It guides us in using our natural and spiritual resources at a time when we need both.

Mourning: The Journey from Grief to Healing, Patrick Del Zoppo, Alba House, 1996. The author explains the mourning process in both an informational and spiritual way, presenting the necessary elements of the healing process with compassion and gentleness.

Hope for Bereaved, Therese Schoeneck, Hope for Bereaved, 1995. This book contains numerous articles to help the reader understand what he or she is going through as the grieving process unfolds.

The Tree That Survived the Winter, Mary Fahy, Paulist Press, 1989. The author presents an allegory that deals with survival and growth after dying and death takes place. A sense of hope and fulfillment runs throughout the book.

The Song of the Redbird, Paula D'Arcy, Crossroad Publishing, 1996. Once we recognize our crisis, there is hope that we can not only overcome it but by reflection and prayer grow spiritually because of it. The author describes her journey of spirit through death to resurrection.

The New Day Journal, rev. ed., Mauryeen O'Brien, ACTA Publications, 2000. This resource is for those going through the initial stages of grief. Written in journal form, it offers a structured approach to dealing with the death of a loved one.

Holiday Help: A Guide for Hope and Healing, Darcie Sims and Sherrie Williams, Accord, 1996. This useful book offers guidance and practical hints on how to get through the holidays after a loved one has died.

How Will I Get Through the Holidays? James Miller, Willowgreen, 1996. Twelve suggestions filled with information concerning moving through the holidays after the death of a loved one.

Prayers

Good Morning, God

Good Morning, God.
You are ushering in another day,
Untouched and freshly new,
So here I come to ask you, God,
If you'll renew me too.

Forgive the many errors
That I made yesterday
And let me try again, dear God,
To walk closer in your way.

But, Father, I am well aware
I can't make it on my own,
So take my hand and hold it tight,
For I cannot walk alone.

(Vincent Marquis)

The Serenity Prayer

God grant me the serenity to accept
things I cannot change,
the courage to change things I can,
and the wisdom to know the difference.

(author unknown)

The Difference

I got up early one morning
and rushed right into the day;
I had so much to accomplish
that I didn't have time to pray.
Problems just tumbled about me,
and heavier came each task.
"Why doesn't God help me?" I wondered.
God answered, "You didn't ask."
I wanted to see joy and beauty,
but the day toiled on, gray and bleak;
I wondered why God didn't show me.
God said, "But you didn't seek."
I tried to come into God's presence;
I used all my keys at the lock.
God gently and lovingly chided,
"My child, you didn't knock."
I woke up early this morning,
and paused before entering the day.
I had so much to accomplish
that I had to take time to pray.

(author unknown)

Psalm 23

The LORD is my shepherd, I shall not want.
     He makes me lie down in green pastures;
he leads me beside still waters;
     he restores my soul.
He leads me in right paths
     for his name's sake.

Even though I walk through the darkest valley,
     I fear no evil;
for you are with me;
     your rod and your staff—
     they comfort me.

You prepare a table before me
>   in the presence of my enemies;
you anoint my head with oil;
>   my cup overflows.
Surely goodness and mercy shall follow me
>   all the days of my life,
and I shall dwell in the house of the LORD
>   my whole life long.

Psalm 130

Out of the depths I cry to you, O LORD.
>   LORD, hear my voice!
Let your ears be attentive
>   to the voice of my supplications!

If you, O LORD, should mark iniquities,
>   Lord, who could stand?
But there is forgiveness with you,
>   so that you may be revered.

I wait for the LORD, my soul waits,
>   and in his word I hope;
my soul waits for the LORD
>   more than those who watch for the morning,
>   more than those who watch for the morning.

O Israel, hope in the LORD!
>   For with the LORD there is steadfast love,
>   and with him is great power to redeem.
It is he who will redeem Israel
>   from all its iniquities.

Prayer of the Bereaved

We give our loved ones back to you, Lord,
as you gave them to us.

As you did not lose in the giving,
neither do we lose them in the return.

What you give,
you never really take away.

What is yours is always ours also,
if we are yours.

Life is eternal, Lord,
and your love is undying.

Death is only a horizon,
and a horizon is nothing but the limits of our sight.

Lift us up, strong Son of God,
on that same cross on which you were raised,
so that we may see farther.

Open our eyes,
as you opened the eyes of the man born blind,
so that we may see more clearly.

Draw us closer to yourself,
as you drew the little children to you,
so that we may be closer to our loved ones
who are with you.

While you prepare a place for them,
prepare us to live without them for a while.

Amen.

(author unknown)

A Gaelic Blessing

Deep peace
of the running wave to you
deep peace of the flowing air to you
deep peace of the quiet earth to you

Deep peace of the shining stars to you
deep peace of the gentle night to you
moon and stars,
pour their healing light on you
deep peace to you.

(author unknown)

Acknowledgments

I am grateful to Dr. J. William Worden, whose writings on the "Four Tasks of Mourning" have been a constant inspiration for me.

Special gratitude to Cecelia O'Brien for her contribution to the assembly of this text, to Gregory Pierce of ACTA Publications, who encouraged me to write it, and to John Van Bemmel, who applied his editing skills to the manuscript.

Additional Grief Resources

The New Day Journal, Revised Version
A Journey from Grief to Healing
Mauryeen O'Brien, O.P.

A structured approach to facing the death of a loved one, based on the belief that writing and sharing one's thoughts, feelings and experiences is one of the most helpful ways to move beyond pain and loss. Can be used by individuals or in a bereavement support group. (93-page workbook, ISBN: 0-87946-130-6, $9.95)

The Death of a Husband
Reflections for a Grieving Wife
Helen Reichert Lambin

A collection of poignant reflections for any wife mourning the loss of her husband. Over forty stories, remembrances, meditations and poems consider the different facets of the grieving process. (128-page paperback, ISBN: 0-87946-179-9, $8.95)

The Death of a Wife
Reflections for a Grieving Husband
Robert L. Vogt

Reflections and meditations that touch the heart and point out new and hopeful directions for any grieving husband. Each of the thirty-one brief chapters touches on a different issue faced by a husband who has lost his wife. (112-page paperback, ISBN: 0-897946-141-1, $8.95)

Always Precious in Our Memory
Reflections after Miscarriage, Stillbirth or Neonatal Death
Kristen Johnson Ingram

Over seventy heartfelt meditations address the powerful emotions felt by parents who have endured the death of a baby. Each brief reflection—combined with a carefully chosen Scripture quotation—will help parents, family members and friends understand the grief, regret, anger and guilt they are feeling. (96-page paperback, ISBN: 0-87946-159-4, $8.95)

Available from Christian book sellers or call 800-397-2282.